The radically changi

WORK, WORKERS & WORKPLACES

Using space as the starting point of innovation

PARTHAJEET SARMA

Become
Shakespeare
.com

First published in 2018 by

Becomeshakespeare.com
Wordit Content Design & Editing Services Pvt Ltd
Unit - 26, Building A-1, Nr Wadala RTO,
Wadala (East),
Mumbai 400037, India
T:+91 8080226699

This book has been funded by WORDIT ART FUND
WORDIT ART FUND helps deserving
Authors publish their work
To apply for funding, please visit us at
becomeshakespeare.com

©
ISBN : 978-93-87649-97-2

Disclaimer
This is a work of nonfiction. No names have been changed,
no characters invented, no events fabricated. However, the
author has relied on others for some of the information,
and has tried his best to ensure the authenticity of such
information. Such information cannot be vouched for.
Although the author is a management consultant, he is not
your consultant yet. Reading this work of nonfiction, does
not create a consultant-client relationship between you
and the author.

OTHER BOOKS BY THE AUTHOR

- *Smart Phones, Dumb People?*
- *The Rich Labourer*

DEDICATION

To all those who inspired this book, and will not read it.

SPECIAL THANKS

Thanks to the team at www.emporiomdigital.com for introducing me to Amazon Alexa and all things digital tech from the day I became an author.

Thank you Alexa for keeping my kids busy while I wrote this and for making me believe that anything is possible.

Huge thanks to my wife for making everything possible. Thank God her parents did not name her Alexa!

Lastly many thanks to John Hoffmire at the University of Oxford for believing in me for everything I do, including the seemingly impossible.

AUTHOR INTRODUCTION

Parthajeet Sarma is a Chevening scholar (University of Oxford), award-winning innovator and entrepreneur. Fifteen out of his over two decades of work experience has been as an entrepreneur. Set up in 2003 by Parthajeet, iDream has metamorphosed to be a boutique strategic management consultancy, handholding change management in corporate organizations.

Besides iDream, Parthajeet also acts as an advisor at Gallopper. Gallopper fuels experimentation and discourses around design as the core in business transformation. Parthajeet's experimentation efforts have yielded award winning products and services. He is a winner of The Economic Times 'Power of Ideas' 2012, Sankalp Awards for social innovation and others. He has been featured across various electronic and print media including CNBC TV-18's 'Young Turks'.

A graduate of Sir J J College of Architecture, Mumbai, Parthajeet went on to complete an MBA. After years of industry experience, he was selected by the British Government to do a leadership program on science and innovation at the University of Oxford. Husband to a fellow professional and a father of two daughters, Parthajeet is a regular speaker at industry forums as well as in educational institutions.

www.parthajeet.com

TABLE OF CONTENTS

INTRODUCTION

Over the last decade and half we have engaged our boutique consultancy iDream and myself in more and more collaborative work. Today, on an average, over 50% of the resources devoted on our assignments, comprise of professionals who are project specific collaborators and not on the payroll of iDream. This is a distinct shift from our beginnings in 2003 when more than 90% of project resources were sourced internally. This has allowed us to drastically reduce our costs, increase profitability and more importantly, to be able to deliver highly focused services.

This is reflective of the way we have changed over the last fifteen years from managing one part of client's business needs, i.e. office fit-outs, to becoming a niche strategic consultant where we need to immerse ourselves deeply into the heart of the client organization. With the radically changing nature of work, workers and workplaces, today we handhold organizations as they begin to use the workplace as the starting point of innovation. To do this, we need to collaborate and bring together a wider and richer network of professionals who can contribute to a holistic, collaborative approach towards solving client problems.

Secondly this is also reflective of the way the world has changed over the last 15 years, as collaborations between business houses and between entrepreneurs become more commonplace. Easy telecommunications has made it possible to access resources from any part of the world. It is not surprising to find project teams comprising of members from three different countries, servicing a client in a fourth country.

When we had refurbished our office in 2014, we built a meeting room and a nice huddle area within it. This was meant for internal meetings as well as for client meetings. Similarly the workplaces of our clients and collaborators have beautiful meeting places. However most of my meetings today happen in coffee shops, and rarely at our workplace or at the workplace of the other party that we are meeting. Coffee shops serve as neutral ground for meetings and bring about a sense of equality. Moreover, the sights and smells of a coffee shop allow human connections to be built far more easily than within the sterile confines of a boardroom. I have struck many a business deal in coffee shops.

This is true for many others. More and more business meetings among entrepreneurs and executives are happening in coffee shops and in newer forms of eateries. Walk into a Starbucks and it is not surprising to see more laptops than coffee mugs on the tables. This is akin to early signs of a paradigm shift. A paradigm shift is a fundamental change in an individual's or a society's view of how things work in the world. For example, the shift from earth to sun as the center of the solar system or heart to brain as the seat of thinking and feeling. The result of a paradigm shift, like in the case of a Starbucks visit, is people changing the meaning for which they do certain things. Not too long ago, eateries and coffee shops were places you went to for a coffee or for a meal. But today, a lot of business deals are struck in such places. The meaning of going to a coffee shop has changed.

A paradigm shift does not occur in isolation and influences society as a whole. The global economy shifted from manufacturing to services around the middle of the twentieth century. Later, as the economy began to absorb more and more researchers, engineers and designers to invent new products and improve processes, the next shift was to a knowledge economy, as organizations began to invest in research labs and the brightest of human talents. However, with a smartphone in everyone's hands today, a young twenty something worker could have far greater access to knowledge than a senior manager would have had one generation back. With a lot of the knowledge related work being automated, the one important skill, high in demand for humans today, is to be able to do things machines cannot; that is, work effectively with other humans. The ability to collaborate with humans as well as with machines is the competitive advantage, as knowledge workers become relationship workers. So, while the coffee gets cold on the side, a visit to a Starbucks is really about collaboration with humans and machines. The world has shifted from a knowledge economy to a collaboration economy.

Technology aids in the shift, sometimes unknowingly, as people adapt to new meanings behind doing things. Free wifi allow people to have business meetings in coffee shops. VR technology enables new gaming consoles to allow life-like experiential activity. However, the invention of a new technology itself does not necessarily lead to immediate commercial gain or social impact. Often it is seen that a newly discovered technology sits inside the lab for many years before someone finds an application for it, leading to a product, which changes the way we live. For example, the first 3D printers were available for commercial use in 1988; however it took nearly three decades before this invention got to the tipping point. Earlier owned mainly by research and design departments of a few large-scale product manufacturers, it is only now that core technology advancements and affordability is helping 3D printers make inroads amongst smaller organizations. We are still a few years away from it being adopted by each and every startup and entrepreneur who needs it.

The entire eco-system required for new technology adoption needs to be ready before products and services based on the new technology can be successful. Sometimes it takes decades and sometimes it takes just months. An app based business idea like on-demand taxi service provider Uber became popular very fast as the eco-system was ready with the platform, cars, drivers and customers. Almost overnight, it shifted the ground beneath the foundation of conventional transportation businesses built around privately owned vehicles and around regular taxis. The paradigm shifted, as millions saw greater value in Uber over car ownership, especially in crowded cities with parking problems.

With wifi becoming as basic as water & electricity and with newer technologies like AI and VR, it is but obvious that tens of thousands of examples of application of such technology will be seen in the coming years. While a majority of such innovative products and services may fail to find a liking, a few will stick and will change the way we live and the meaning behind doing some things as humans.

Without much realization, humans are slowly but surely adopting newer meanings behind doing things that they do. The meaning behind going to a coffee shop has changed. The meaning behind visiting a bank has changed. Ever since the introduction of ATMs, the need to visit a bank for withdrawing money has evaporated. One visits a bank today only for select services which require purely human skills; and this has led banks to launch new services around insurance and investments to keep customers engaged. With online and mobile banking gaining currency, the need to go to an ATM is drastically reduced. As the meaning behind doing things change, humans change in the way they live. Their expectations from things and experiences change, their expectations from family changes. Their expectations from work change.

We are staring at a world where driverless electric transportation systems are beginning to transport people from place to place. With the need for drivers disappearing, the transportation industry will undergo tectonic changes. With reduced need for fossil fuels in transportation, the oil industry will be disrupted. New types of jobs will be created, as the very meaning of 'going to work' will change.

In fact, the very nature of work has changed drastically over the last two decades. Till twenty years back, it was about going to a workplace, sitting at a desk for eight hours, doing the assigned work and returning home, and then spending time with family. Family life was far removed from work life and there was much talk about finding a balance between the two. However the two aspects of life are integrated today, as we carry our work in our pockets, in our cellphones and on our laptops. Work happens as much in trains and in coffee shops, as they do in boardrooms. Work life and family life are integrated.

It is not unrealistic to ask "Why do I need to go to my workplace?". This is one question that organizations increasingly will have to answer as HR managers debate on the merits of remote working. One of the big challenges that organizations face today is attracting the right talent and a bigger challenge is to retain them. Organizations need to do things differently today to attract and retain talent. The twentieth century carrot and stick methods have failed to give results in the twenty first century as motivation for doing things have changed at a fundamental level for people.

Secondly a lot of the work, which were being done by humans in the twentieth century, has been automated.

Computer programs and apps are doing most of the repetitive, left-brained, logical kind of work today. Humans are mostly left with right brained, creative work, which require skills, which are essentially human.

So, not only is our working environment changing rapidly, but even the nature of 'work' itself is changing. Twenty years back, white collared workers mostly used to sit within a physical workplace for eight hours, doing repetitive work. Today, as white collared workers juggle between emails, spreadsheets and videoconferences, they work within an environment that is a blend of physical and digital spaces, doing work that is relatively non-repetitive. The new workplace is a blended space of the physical and the digital.

Organizations need to realize and adapt to this new reality of blended workplaces quickly, if they want their workers to continue to work for them. The inspiration for coming to work today is drastically different from that of the nineties. Running an organization with a twenty-first century sounding mission statement, but from a workplace, which is reflective of a twentieth-century legacy, could be a disaster waiting to happen.

Global corporations like Google and Apple have successfully managed to align the organization's vision with the blended spaces that their workers, and even their clients experience. Apple products have boasted about simplicity and have raised it to a level of sophistication. In line with this ethos, when you walk in to any Apple store, simplicity is at display everywhere.

From the way products are displayed, to the fact that no customer is 'bothered' by salesmen. You can experience the products by yourself and ask for help if you need any, as you transit between the digital and physical worlds. Any Apple staff can check you out with no dedicated checkout counter. It is a blended space, very similar to an iPhone, which is a mix of a physical product and services. The experience in an Apple store is not very different from the experience of using an iPhone. Similarly the new Apple campus in California reflects the same ideology.

Organizations spend millions of dollars in trying to understand their consumers, markets and new technology, so that they can come up with better products, and stay ahead of competition. In today's collaboration economy, the most popular buzzword is innovation and its various forms. In such an economy, the biggest investment is into an organization's workers, and not into machines. However, relatively less effort goes into understanding the needs and aspirations of the workers. What motivates them? What drives them? Unless people are inspired, it is hard to expect quality work from them.

The second biggest investment for any organization is usually into real estate to house the workers. As the physical space within which workers work becomes augmented with technology, it is of paramount importance for organizations to adapt to a new form of blended workplaces, which allow workers to remain inspired and innovative.

This book is about the changing nature of work, workers and workplaces. It is about the new blended workplace, and how that can be used as the starting point of innovation. It is about what inspires workers today, about the changing nature of HR and finally about how organizations can make this transition as the ground beneath them shifts. What this book is not about, is a 3 step process or about a codified way of adopting a new management theory. Although management likes codified processes like Six Sigma and Design Thinking, such processes are limiting in the sense that sooner or later everyone adopts it, and one finds oneself not being distinctively different from the other. Codified management theories are remnants of the twentieth century thinking, which allowed measurement of outputs in tangible quantities. The collaboration economy of the twenty first century needs management to break away from a codified mentality, start thinking and build upon their unique strengths. This book helps such thinking to begin.

The book has three broad sections: Section 1 highlights what the topic is all about. Section 2 highlights why it is so very important, and the last Section 3 shows the path forward.

SECTION 1: What is it all about?

In early 2018, an old friend proudly invited me to take a look at their swanky new workplace in a prime business district of Mumbai. He is at senior management level in an American multinational corporation. He took me around the space during a working day, showing me every corner of the new workplace. With commercial real estate prices in Mumbai at stratospheric levels, the new design was pretty bold, especially given that they had built in several people centric spaces like huddle areas, thinking pods, coffee points, telephone booths, gym, yoga room and the like. With video-conferencing rooms, wifi across the workplace and even a virtual reality room, workers can transit seamlessly from the physical to digital space. A few years back, such spaces would have been looked upon as non-productive frills and a waste of expensive real estate. It was encouraging to note that most of these new spots were being populated and being used for impromptu meetings and phone calls.

The science is out there to demonstrate that blended workplaces work well. The cubicle farms of the last century are passé. Workplaces of today need to have a

1

wide variety of spaces, which allow workers to work in isolation at times, collaborate when necessary and recharge as well. Workers are different from each other and different types of people find comfort in different types of settings. Moreover, different types of work require different types of settings. Accountants need to be number focused, whereas marketing professionals need to collaborate and communicate. One size does not fit all like in the industrial era. So a workplace that allows opportunities for all types of people to flourish is good for the organization's bottom line. In Section 2, I will deal with this aspect in detail.

So my visit to my friend's new workplace was a refreshing change to observe. They seemed to have adapted to the new age philosophy of blended workplaces. After a fifteen-minute stroll around the workplace, we began to look for a place to sit and have a coffee. All of the informal meeting areas seemed occupied. There was only one of the four formal meeting rooms free, and we went in. Then something strange happened. We had to book the meeting room and there was a touch screen on the door to do that. The screen informed us that the room was available for thirty minutes. So we booked the room. As soon as the room was booked, the door unlocked itself and a countdown timer started. It was counting down to thirty minutes. As we sat down, another screen inside reminded us that we had twenty-nine minutes left to finish the meeting.

The technological suaveness was enviable. However, as the clocked ticked by, we found ourselves looking at the countdown every few minutes to check how much time we were left with. A small beep warned us when we had only five minutes left and another warned us when we had two minutes left. We left before it hit zero and as we exited, we saw two ladies waiting outside. They seemed to have booked the room for the next session.

I do not have much recollection of what we spoke about during those thirty minutes. The proverbial sword hanging over our heads burdened our conversation; the mind was preoccupied with the thought that we had to finish whatever we were doing in thirty minutes.

I found the countdown panel to be a complete contradiction to the open, innovative culture, which the design of the furniture and spaces seemed to propagate. The new workplace had no offices, except one for the Managing Director. The workplace was a welcoming openness of workstations, huddle areas, cafeterias, beanbags, greenery, viewing gallery, a gym and what not. One could operate from anywhere that one wanted to. So, on one hand, the workplace spelled friendliness, openness, collaboration and looked like a great place for ideation; but on the other hand you had a piece of modern technology, which seemed to be barring ideation and freedom.

Technology has been a great boon. Digital technology has taken the world by storm from the beginning of the current millennium. There is a general belief that stuff like internet of things, 3D printing, cloud computing, personalized medicine, alternative energy and virtual reality and their application can disrupt businesses and improve lives. To some extent it has. When one leading business house adopts any new digital technology to improve some of its business processes, usually competitors are quick to follow with a slight variant of the same technology. This is akin to you buying the latest digital tool. When you buy it, you feel on top of the world. But soon everyone around you has what you have, and then the novelty evaporates. The first mover usually adopts new technology aligned with its core vision, and gets value delivered from the adoption. However blind adoption of the same technology by others, without an alignment with the organization's vision is unlikely to deliver value.

In context of my friend's new workplace, the smart piece of technology on the door appeared out of sync, and not in line with the apparent vision to be open and innovative as an organization. Blind application of digital technology has no benefit, and at times may even be dangerous. Everyday we see new apps being launched by members of the 'Anything-which-is-offline-can-be-made-online Club'. Ninety-nine out of a hundred such launches fail. If you come across a piece of great technology, which may or may not have seen application in business, blind application of it in your business is not going to help, just because the base technology is great. Technology is not our greatest savior. It can only aid business processes if its application is relevant in the given context and if it is integrated with the organization's vision.

Given the way the world is changing so fast, organizations often introspect and re-invent themselves in an effort to stay relevant. A change in vision is often translated into business process changes and cosmetic changes like change of logo, change of workplace design. However, a real re-invention can happen when the entire eco-system is overhauled holistically; with an approach to enable change management through complementary elements including technologies, services, standards, facilities and regulations. Only then will each element deliver on their value proposition. While adopting new technology, it is important to assess whether it can satisfy user needs and deliver value in a better way.

While LED bulbs found instant application and delivered value to users, HDTV took nearly thirty years to be adopted. The former had an ecosystem, which was ready. In case of HDTVs the supporting eco-system was not ready as HD cameras, new broadcast standards, post-production processes were not yet readily available. In a similar manner, at my friend's new workplace and elsewhere, a new piece of technology which instilled rigid discipline will stick out like a sore thumb if the surrounding environment otherwise propagated creativity, innovation and collaboration.

IT departments in organizations came into being only thirty years back. Larger organizations have facilities departments, which look after the planning and management of the physical infrastructure like real estate required to house and run the organization.

Smaller organizations usually get the administration department to run this function. Then there is the HR department, which sometimes works in tandem with the facilities department or the administration team, when it comes to the planning of facilities. These departments, along with the accounts team, are often seen as 'support functions' and relegated to the back of the workplace. Each department is treated as independent units with very little conversation and co-ordination between them.

With IT becoming the backbone of organizations and our personal lives, it can very well stop being a support function and work as the great integrator. It is about time that management looked at an integrated approach to deliver value to its workers and its customers. A 'buying off the shelves' approach to IT and other support services is not only a waste of time and money, but can be disastrous. An integrated approach is the order of the day.

Solutions at the periphery

Although the organization where my friend works may have failed in integrating technology in the right context of the playful nature of the new workplace, the workplace design on its own is reflective of the changing aspirations of the twenty first century white collared worker. New age thinking allows playfulness to be incorporated into workplace designs. Workplaces need to be a combination of different types of blended spaces, where workers can seamlessly go from a playful mode to a collaborative mode. 'Play' however, is not to be read as an activity; 'play' in this context is a mindset. Putting basketball rings and a TT table in a workplace is meaningless if the management approach is one of strict control. I will explain the positive impacts of incorporating play in modern workplaces in Section 2. Let me elaborate on the need to do so with the example of an experiment.

This is the candle problem experiment, and was first conducted in 1945. The experimenters got a few participants to come into a room and gave them a bunch of things to work with; i.e., a candle, some drawing pins and some matchsticks. Pic 1 is demonstrative of the way the items were presented. The participants were asked to attach the candle to the wall in a manner such that the wax does not drip onto the table, when the candle is lit.

Pic 1

How would you do it? Look at the image and think about it for a couple of minutes.

What do you think?

A few of the participants in the experiment tried to nail the candle to the wall with the drawing pins, but were unsuccessful. The wax would still drip onto the table. A few melted the side of the candle and stuck it to the wall. It still did not work. Finally, after a few minutes of deliberation, they come up with the solution, which is shown in Pic 2. The box holding the pins was used as a stand to hold the candle. Slowly, people had overcome pattern thinking and functional fixedness. At first look, the box looks like a container for the drawing pins. But if you change the perspective, you realize that it can also have other uses as well. It can be the platform for the candle.

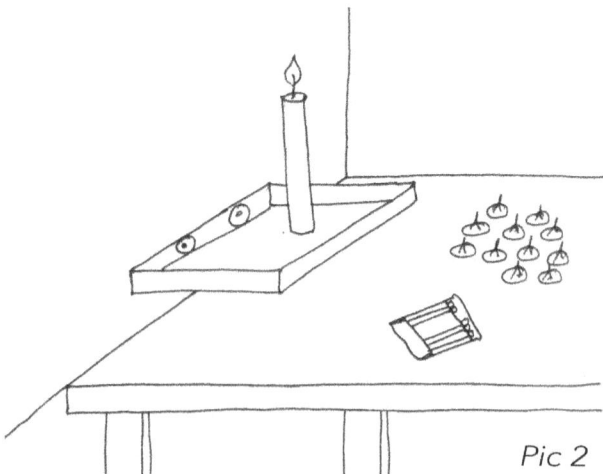

Pic 2

Then they took the experiment one step further, in order to study the effect of incentives on performance. This time, the experimenters divided the participants into two groups. The same items were shown to the two groups with the same aim. However the rules were slightly different for each group. The first group was told that they would be timed to see how long they take to solve the problem, in an effort to establish the average time taken to solve the problem. On the other hand, the second group was offered rewards, for finishing fast. The fastest twenty five percent amongst the participants would get fifty dollars each, and the fastest would get two hundred dollars. (I adjusted the numbers to take inflation into consideration.) Now, those appear to be attractive numbers for a few minutes of work. If we want workers to perform well, we incentivize them, right?

The biggest surprise from this variant of the experiment was that, on an average, the incentivized group took three and a half minutes longer to solve the problem. So when an incentive was designed to sharpen thinking and accelerate creativity, it was doing just the opposite. Creativity was getting blocked and thinking was dulled. The same variant of the experiment, when repeated today, gives the same results. A carrot and stick approach where we tell people "if you do this, you get that", work in certain conditions but for a lot of tasks, they actually don't work, or in some cases, they do harm. This has been one of the most profound social science findings. But sadly this is one of the most ignored as well. Even today, most of our businesses are built around a 'carrot and stick' approach. This is fine for many kinds of twentieth century tasks where output can be measured on the factory floor in tangible numbers. But in the collaboration economy of the twenty first century, which calls for creative thinking, this approach does not work.

So, do incentives never work? Well, they do; in certain conditions. The candle problem has a third variant, which gives a clue about conditions in which incentives work well.

The experimenters got the participants into two groups again. But this time they presented the items in a slightly different way; the drawing pins were left out of their containers. Look at Pic 3. Both the groups were given the same task, to attach the candle to the side of the wall so that wax does not drip onto the table, when the candle is lit. One group was being watched for

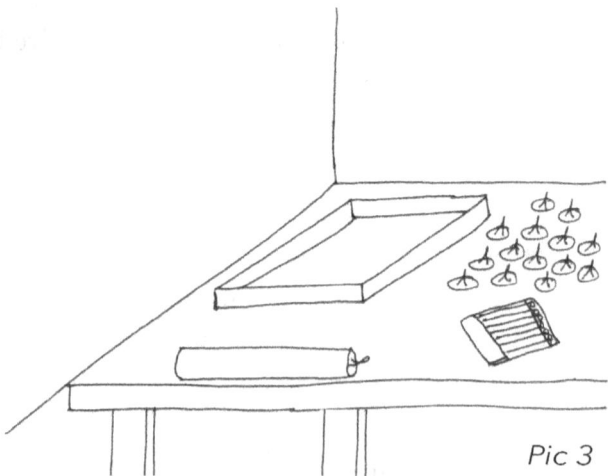

Pic 3

norms and the other was incentivized. Guess what happened this time?

This time, the incentivized group defeated the other group. So, when the pins are out of the container, it is easy, is it not? It indicates that incentives work really well for those kind of tasks, where there is a simple set of rules and there is a clear destination to go to. Incentives and rewards narrow our focus and help the mind concentrate; so they work in cases like this. In our day-to-day lives, in tasks with a simple set of rules where the destination is visible, we quickly get to the destination. But unfortunately such tasks are hard to come by. The solutions, if any, to problems we face in the twenty first century are on the periphery. So one ought to be looking around and not be bound by pressures of time and incentives. Monetary incentives for time bound activities narrow our focus and restricts our possibilities.

Why is this important?

All over the world, white collared workers are doing less and less of left-brained, logical, repetitive work, and more of complex right brained kind of work; which requires one's cognitive skills to be at the forefront. Routine, rule based work involving accounting, financial analysis and certain kinds of administrative work, have mostly been automated. Computers can do it faster and without errors. So what really matter in the twenty first century are the right brained, creative, conceptual kinds of abilities. At my workplace and at yours, the problems that we face usually do not have a clear set of rules and a clear destination. The rules are hazy and the solution is often surprising and definitely not obvious.

So when we are dealing with this kind of candle problems today, the workplaces of today need to be reflective of such a commitment of management's understanding of the changed environment. Workplaces need to facilitate the mind to wander, to play, to collaborate and allow social and neural connections to happen.

Our working tools are in our hands

The concept of 'going to work' was introduced in a formal manner with the dawn of the industrial revolution, when workers began to work in factories. The industrial revolution also gave us the assembly line, and the assembly line was all about productivity and efficiency. There was no room for error. The concept of going to a workplace for work is a natural extension of going to the factory. The first workplaces were designed with rows and rows of workstations, with a manager overlooking performance, almost mimicking the factory shop floor. Later on, there was a feeling that the workstation farms did not offer any privacy, so cubicles were introduced.

Then something happened to us. The internet happened, and then came smart phones. Then came all the new digital technology. And this changed the paradigm completely. People no more needed to go to work; they began carrying their work in their pockets. Earlier the 'tools of work' were at the factory shop floor and later at the workplace. Now the tools are in the cloud and on the smartphones. So today, the big challenge that organizations face is that people do not 'need to' come to work anymore. Workers can work from home, from trains and from coffee shops.

Instead of debating the merits of working from home vs. the demerits of it, one needs to look at the benefits of working from home or from a coffee shop and explore the possibility of incorporating such benefits at the workplace. This is what has led to the emergence of a discourse on the need for workplaces to be more 'homely' and playful, mimicking many of the benefits one usually gets 'outside of work'. The Fortune 'list of best organizations to work for', have workplaces that today look like clubs; where workers can get a sauna, go for a jog, play a game of snooker, sleep and work from a café or from a bean bag.

THE CHANGING NATURE OF WORK

Along with work, workers and workplaces are changing. Although change is not new, the rate of change is way faster than what we have seen in the past.

Work, workers and workplaces have seen drastic change at different points in history and have also attracted unrest and protests. In the nineteenth century, the Luddites, a group of English textile workers and weavers, destroyed weaving machinery as a form of protest. They feared that the time spent learning the skills of their craft would go to waste, as machines would replace their role in the industry.

Two hundred years down the line, there is much similarity in the discourse around robots taking over our jobs. One school of thought says that automation will kill jobs and humans will have nothing to do. This is rather far fetched. In the history of mankind, it has never been a 'them or us' situation. Machines have always augmented human life.

A major difference between the Luddites movement and the current discourse around Man vs. Machine is that, this time around, humans will be left to do more and more of right-brained creative work, as left brained repetitive work is taken over by machines. Human work will revolve around thinking creatively, using emotional intelligence, making value judgement, communicating and teaching.

The question is not about job loss, but about certain activities within a job being taken over by machines. Activities are vulnerable to automation. So work, workers and workplaces will change. A radically new concept of workplaces will play a significant role in shaping the changing nature of work and workers. Thinking workers will need to welcome innovation as an inherent part of their work. This book is about using the workplace as the starting point of innovation.

Human careers are today being shaped around learning and not around jobs, as shelf life of business competency drops rapidly. The new mix of talents and skills at the diverse workplace includes regular workers, freelancers, crowd-sourced talent, working harmoniously with robots and AI applications.

As every job is getting reinvented, it is giving rise to an augmented workforce working in an augmented workplace. The new workplace is not a physical space anymore, but a combination of the physical and the digital. Organizations ought to reconsider the very meaning of workplace design to incorporate redesign of jobs and organize work as they plan for future growth.

The new kind of work will revolve around what are essentially human skills. Skills such as empathy, communication, persuasion, personal service, problem solving, and strategic decision making are more valuable than ever. Automation will help redefine jobs, boost productivity, and allow workers to focus on the human aspects of work.

During a recent visit to a bank, I found the teller advising me on certain new investment plans. After much persuasion over coffee, I agreed to a plan. To execute the financial plan that I selected, I needed to log on to the bank's app on my phone and send instructions digitally. In a few seconds I received a message on my phone indicating that the transaction was done.

The teller in a bank hardly doles out cash today, but works seamlessly in a blended space of the physical and the digital. He or she switches roles with ease; acting as a financial advisor with one customer and as a fire-fighter with another who may be experiencing problems with the bank's mobile app. The skills required from such a job are those, which cannot be performed by machines; i.e. essentially human skills requiring empathy. This is true of other industry segments as well, as humans begin to work as collaborators between other fellow humans and machines. Organizations are today faced with the challenge to redesign workplaces, which allow such collaboration to happen. Such digitally infused workplaces tend to be more open, collaborative, yet provide opportunities for development, growth and focus time. Successful organizations will be those that have enough open, collaborative physical and digital spaces to facilitate people-to-people meetings and collaboration. An augmented workforce will work in a completely new kind of workplace. Such a workplace will have a profound influence on the productivity of thinking humans. The next section touches upon the different ways that a workplace can impact human performance.

SECTION 2: Why is it important?

THE POWER OF PLACE

From the days of the industrial era, business owners and leaders have chased productivity, for it is that one thing that keeps the numbers going. In the industrial era, productivity was fuelled by efficiency. In the collaboration economy of today, productivity is largely fueled by creativity, especially if the workplace environment is developed and nurtured in a way that allows the two to peacefully co-exist. In the post Steve Jobs world, it is well established that creativity spells success. Allowing workers time to smell the roses and be creative can lead to increased workplace productivity.

While researching for this book, I came across the results of various social science experiments like the candle problem that I wrote about in the earlier section. There are numerous studies out there, including recent brain imaging studies, which help define factors that boost human creativity. Most of these studies however seem to be gathering dust in untouched corners of libraries with near zero application in building new workplaces. The art and science of building great workplaces, which boost human creativity, seem far removed from the world of human psychology.

The most obvious reason for this is that till recently, there was no need for organizations to think about psychology or social science when it came to workplaces. The modern workplace, like I explained before, is an extension of the factory floor and all that mattered was about efficiency leading to higher productivity; about tangible numbers being achieved. But then, the world changed and it was no more about 'doing the things right' only, but also about 'doing the right things.' Skills, which are purely human, began to matter. Feelings began to matter. Earlier it did not matter if an employee had a breakoff with her boyfriend. It had limited or zero impact on productivity. Today, it matters.

Today organizations are beginning to realize that employee happiness equals a positive bottom-line. Forward thinking organizations are spending time and money to keep their workers happy and part of this plan includes building workplaces which allow them to be at their creative best. Happiness breeds creativity and vice versa.

We have been fortunate to have worked closely with some of the names on Fortune's list of 'World's Best Workplaces' list like Diageo, DHL, Cisco and others. A close look tells you that such organizations invest heavily on workplace happiness. In many of these organizations, offices have been abolished, workers get free meals, have access to games, fitness and wellness rooms within the workplace. Power naps are encouraged; kids can stay in on-site day-care centres. A variety of seating and working options are made available. In most cases, such investment has paid back in terms of lower retention costs and highly engaged workers, which lead to higher profitability.

Interestingly, most organizations featured on the annual 'World's Best Workplaces' list also happen to be top performers in stock markets. The science is out there to show that happier workplaces lead to better financial performance. That is the power of place.

SPACE AND INNOVATION

Creativity is the nature of creating something new. Usage of that creativity to enhance the performance of a process, person, team or organization is what innovation is all about. Creativity and innovation need to co-exist for business success. Innovative organizations realize that innovation stems from creative workers. Creative workers lead new product development and enable new clients to be won. Organizations use innovation as the driving force to increase market share, out-maneuver competition and overcome challenges.

Studies in recent times have demonstrated that there is a direct link between space and creativity. Height, colour, sound, light and the way a space is laid out, can shape the environment that one is in, and the environment shapes one's thinking. Given that an organization has different departments with people doing different types of works, it is important to understand the impact of different types of environments on work. Creativity for a designer is quite different from creativity for an accountant; one size does not fit all.

I had mentioned in Section 1 that many of my meetings happen at coffee shops. The buzz of a coffee shop with the sound of voices, light music and cutlery is a breeding ground for collaborative work. So much so, that on YouTube you will find coffee shop ambient soundtracks that you can download. Some organizations play such soundtracks through ceiling speakers in those areas of the workplace, where collaborative work takes place. When the mind has a slight distraction in the form of background noise, the brain processes information abstractly and this aids creative thinking.

On the other hand, an environment with such background noise does not suit a team of accountants who need to focus on numbers. Such professionals will be able to perform better in a quiet room. Stillness can be unsettling but it makes one more alert to any stimuli. Hearing levels go up in a silent environment, human hearing having evolved over generations by way of detecting predators in the stillness of the Savanna or the dark. This allows one to focus and enhances performance. At the same time, such an environment may be detrimental to any task, which requires creative thinking; wherein the brain needs to be more open to be able to process information abstractly.

While proofreading a print of this book on plain paper, I have chosen to work during the wee hours of the morning with a red pen in my hand. The stillness of the night helps the mind to focus, and the red pen was helpful in catching the typo errors. Our brains associate the colour red with alarms, blood and stop signs. Seeing the colour red stimulates the brain to become more sensitive to failure. So while red works well for proofreading, studies have shown that it can have adverse effects while performing tasks of strategic nature, which calls for big picture thinking.

During an assignment with a like-minded client, we did a small experiment to gauge the effect of height on creative abilities. There is a general belief that high ceilings enhance the creative abilities; we wanted to test this hypothesis. The client organization played along and we designed a test with questions on abstract thinking. We were given a bunch of willing workers and on a Saturday we divided the bunch into two groups. We asked each group to take the same test in two different rooms. Both the rooms were identical except that one room had a ceiling, which was higher by two feet. We hung some paper mobiles from the respective ceilings to make sure that the ceiling was noticed. The results were telling. Individual scores, on an average, were higher in the room with the higher ceiling. Places with higher ceilings enable us to think more freely. We are usually more creative when ceilings are higher. At the same time we feel crowded and want people to stay away from us when the ceiling is less than nine feet.

Unlike 'Stop' and 'Walk' signs for pedestrians, the brain does not need to be told how to behave as one enters a space. The subconscious mind adjusts human behavior automatically, while the conscious mind is reserved to perform the task at hand. Forward thinking organizations take much care to understand such insights, which aid performance for different types of workers, and explore ways to build workplaces, which allow workers to remain engaged. However the needs of different types of workers are different. Secondly individual needs also change during different times. Opportunities need to be created for collaboration, creative thinking as well as for focused attention. The modern workplace is a blend of these different types of spaces.

THE EVOLUTION OF THE MODERN DAY WORKPLACE

The world is big on collaboration today and the positive role it plays in making innovation successful. While this is true, collaboration is only one part of a collection of things required for innovation success. An open office culture, which allows ample opportunity for human connections to happen, is based on the need to collaborate. Such an 'extroverted' workplace culture is being questioned today, as it may limit focused attention and creative thinking. Workplaces are changing to becoming a blend of a variety of spaces. In the evolution of the workplace over a hundred years, this is not the first time that the open office culture is seeing a change. In some ways, we seem to have come full circle.

The earliest workplaces in the early part of the twentieth century were an extension of the shop floor. Frederic Taylor, a management guru, had a strong influence on workplace culture. His goal was to maximize worker efficiency, akin to the shop floor. Rows and rows of workstations with low or no partitions ensured that everyone was visible and could be monitored. Most of the work done at such desks was logical, repetitive, left-brain kind of work. Air conditioning was introduced in the thirties and fluorescent lighting was introduced in the forties. As the layout of workplaces were no more limited by the need to be near natural light, the workplaces of the fifties saw managers sitting by the windows and the workers in the middle of the room. The cubicle was introduced in the sixties as the issue of privacy came up. The cubicle offered visual privacy, to a growing breed of sales and marketing personnel. Recession and mergers of the eighties and the early nineties saw layoffs and the need to optimize space. Organizations began to cramp in more and more people in a combination of smaller workstations and cubicles.

An insurance company that we worked with in the nineties had seven types of workspaces for seven levels of hierarchies. As one climbed the corporate ladder within this organization, he or she would get a bigger space. At the very top two tiers, one would be boxed inside offices. So, the better you did, the more removed you would be from other colleagues. The most talented executives were being restricted from collaborating with the others in this hierarchy, which is a pity, especially since innovation is said to be fueled by chance encounters. Think about your own work. Chances are very limited that you got your last bright idea while sitting in front of a computer inside a closed room. We went on to recommend trimming their workspace typologies to three from seven. By doing this, not only could they save a whopping 30% on real estate costs, but they also metamorphosed into an organization, which was more collaborative in nature.

As the technological revolution and the dotcom boom took over in the late nineties and the early part of the twenty first century, organizations reverted to open air plans, similar to the layouts in the pre-cubicle era. The high partitions came down as realization dawned that privacy is not only about putting up a visual barrier, but also about sound privacy. It is more disturbing to be subjected to high decibels from surrounding workers whom you cannot see, than to be able to see someone across the workstation. Studies showed that sitting in a cubicle for eight hours facing partitions and being disturbed by a barrage of calls, emails and surrounding voices could be very frustrating and also result in high stress and increased blood pressure. This in turn reduces productivity.

Next, as internet and the cellphone made the world a global village, the discourse changed to embrace a collaboration economy. Project teams began to comprise of people from multiple continents, all linked by digital technology. A backlash against the open-air plans followed, as they hampered creativity, reduced attention spans and reduced productivity. For innovation to take place, an organization cannot strive only on collaboration. The frustration of not being able to do one's individual work due to constant collaboration can be counter productive, as it limits one's ability to collaborate. Communication evolving out of such frustration tends to be artificial in nature. Workers fail to stay engaged.

An 'only open seating' work atmosphere can be distracting, whereas a culture of cubicles and offices can be depressing and limit innovation. How does one build a workplace, which is a blend of various types of spaces, which contributes positively to the bottom-line?

The new workplace of today shatters the concept of fixed seating and allows workers to choose from where and how they want to work. What does it mean for HR?

HR : A NEW MEANING

Modern HR policies are largely based on keeping workers motivated by ensuring that they get the right kind of work matching their talents, and supported by monetary and other benefits. This is incomplete. The conscious mind can work well and tap onto the required cognitive resources only if the subconscious mind finds comfort in the surrounding environment. The surrounding environment is shaped through design. Design indeed matters. However, looking at design through the lenses of an interior designer is too narrow. Design, in this context, is not about styling, but takes a deeper meaning embracing unexplored realms.

Organizations wishing to build workplaces, which can enhance productivity, need to take a holistic view and understand human evolution, psychology and science. HR needs to explore newer perspectives and find new meanings of employee wellness.

It is amusing to see some organizations follow Vastu Shastra and Feng Shui consultants blindly and then requesting interior designers to make sudden changes to plans, despite huge time and cost implications. During numerous discussions with such practitioners, I have observed that some of these proponents have followed ancient science blindly. Part of the advice doled out to clients is out of context and meaningless, given the way human expectations from the workplace has changed in recent times. There is nothing wrong behind such ancient sciences of architecture and design, which are based on basic human needs. There are also few practitioners who are able to decipher them in the right context. Seen in the right context, one realizes the value of understanding the human body and mind.

For example, it is often said that letting in natural light into our homes and workplaces is a good practice. Through various experiments, it has also been demonstrated that workers with regular access to natural light tend to perform better than workers who do not get natural light regularly. In hospitals, it is seen that patients heal faster in conditions that allow them access to natural light. Why so? When sunlight hits the human skin, the human body releases nitric oxide into the blood stream. Nitric oxide acts as a blood thinner, and this helps to reduce blood pressure. Reduced blood pressure helps reduce stress and allows the mind access to more cognitive resources required for performing tasks.

New Delhi's air is one of the most polluted amongst large global cities. Right in the heart of the city lays Paharpur Business Centre, a platinum-rated green building. This rating by the U.S. Green Building Council implies that it is one of the most eco-friendly habitable structures in the city. On an experimental visit to the centre, as I entered the building, a sample of my blood was taken to measure the percentage of my blood oxygen level. It showed around 95%. Paharpur Business Centre makes use of hundreds of plants placed across the premises to generate oxygen and absorb carbon dioxide. Moreover the centre generates additional oxygen from a room full of plants, and pumps this oxygen into various working spaces within the building through ducts.

After an hour inside the premises, another sample was taken. This time the oxygen level had gone up to nearly 100%. An optimal supply of oxygen to the brain helps the brain function better; it is as simple as that. Poor air quality is the reason behind a feeling of drowsiness that strikes us sometimes, all of a sudden. Remember the last time you felt sleepy in the middle of an engaging presentation while being holed inside a conference room? It is quite likely that the room had poor supply of fresh air. It is not surprising that workers operating out of Paharpur Business Centre tend to be highly energetic and productive at work.

Nature can have a very positive impact on the quality of work at the workplace. A view of nature augments cognitive abilities in connecting seemingly unrelated ideas. A 'good view' is often used by property developers, hoteliers and clubs as a hook to sell at a premium. Humans have certain behavioural traits ingrained in them from their ancestors. For the caveman, the vantage point was a cave at an elevated point, which allowed safety as well as an unhindered view of the surroundings. This allowed man to keep track of any impending dangers, from the safety of the cave. Similarly, when Indian kings built forts, many of these were strategically built at an elevated spot to keep an eye on enemy soldiers. Similarly a 'machan' in the jungle offers a view of dangerous animals and offers protection at the same time. Over thousands of years, situations, which offered protection and a view of the surroundings, kept us alive.

Brain imaging studies show that pleasure centres of the brain light up when views of nature are seen, indicating that although we are no more cavemen, humans cannot help but feel happy when viewing landscapes, especially from a point of safety.

It is interesting to note how modern day behavior is shaped by ancestral inheritance. During the prehistoric era, the man in the house used to hunt whereas the woman used to tend after the household. Inside a cave, it was the man's duty to keep an eye on the entrance to the cave, to keep his family safe from predators. Cut to modern day workplaces, and one can observe that in a boardroom, men in general prefer a view of the door, whereas women are relatively more open to sitting with their back to the door. Similarly mafia movies show the mafia lords sitting facing the door, and at home the man at the head of the dining table prefers a view of the door.

In the modern day workplace, where the day is packed with a flurry of emails, deadlines and meetings, stress is a free bi-product. The conscious mind is at work managing such stress. On the other hand, the subconscious mind, evolved over thousands of years, adapts to its surroundings automatically and determines the way thinking takes place. When the sub-conscious mind senses a feeling of safety, more cognitive resources are made available. The ability to connect seemingly unrelated points enhances creativity.

A good twenty-first century approach to building productive workplaces requires a holistic HR approach; embracing an understanding of how the human psyche has evolved and the science around it. This change in approach towards understanding workers as humans will lead organizations to change the very premise of workplace design through the narrow lenses of styling. Doing so will enable the workers to tap onto their cognitive resources more than ever before, thereby paving the path forward towards innovation. Space itself can be a starting point of innovation.

THE FIVE SENSES AND PRODUCTIVITY

Space can be the starting point of innovation. For this to happen organizations need to stop looking at workplace design through the lenses of styling and embrace a holistic view of design through the understanding of human psychology, evolution and science. In Section 3, I share my experiences and write about guidelines on how to do this. Organizations need to get out of the structured style of managing by dividing itself into departments with high boundaries, and step back a little, taking a macro view every now and then. This book is about the need and the way to step back and forth from this position; making the macro and the micro work harmoniously.

At the macro level, the first step for an organization is to identify a new meaning of work, workers and the workplace in context of the organization's vision and business goals. At the second level, organizations need to figure out a general concept of the workplace, based on an understanding of the user needs. Design thinking principles come handy in understanding what workers want, at a basic human level. The evolved concept helps in developing a design direction for the workplace. Out of this, in the third step emerges the actual look and feel of the place. A design direction could be something like 'a collaborative workplace' or 'an open and transparent workplace'. This requires designers to explore facets like ergonomics, styling, engineering, features and technology around the established design direction. Such a design direction is a follow through of the new vision at the macro level, which ties together other aspects of the organization structure as well. When the vision and the workplace are in sync, the workplace becomes a physical manifestation of the core of the organization. When this is achieved, workers work effortlessly, in line with the vision.

At the third step, organizations conventionally work with interior designers, architects and associated consultants. Interior designers and architects are generally trained to design for sight. The entire eco-system, including the awards doled out to designers and architects, revolves around good-looking designs. However, in the context of the millennial worker, a good-looking workplace alone is not inspirational enough. Humans experience things through the five senses of sight, sound, touch, smell and taste. In today's world, design is no more about utility alone or about looks alone; but about the entire experience through all five senses. Design as styling is no more a differentiator, as every other workplace is good looking. Designing workplaces for all five senses can enhance creativity and productivity.

Sight: Although interior designers and architects have a good flair for the right use of colours, an understanding of the basic principles of colour psychology helps. Studies have shown the direct connect between colours and mood; and thereby human behavior. So blue walls can promote tranquility, citrus colours like orange enhances social exchanges. Natural light is a popular request by most corporate organizations and the science is out there, showing a strong relationship between daylight at the workplace and workers' sleep patterns, activity and quality of life, all crucial for productivity.

Sound: Productivity levels can dip by more than 50% from sound pollution at the workplace. Worker focus can be thrown out of gear, if one can hear the voices of others talking on the phone, even if they cannot be seen. This is especially true for work, which requires focus. On the other hand, background noise enhances creativity during collaboration activities. Designers need to balance, ensuring that all spaces within a workplace are not designed with the same sound strategy. The impact of sound can be easily understood from the example of pubs playing fast-paced music. Customers consume more liquor in a short period of time, in sync with the fast pace of the music. On the other hand, fine dine restaurants play slow music, as diners linger around for longer periods of time over multiple course meals.

Touch: Although tactile design is a much-studied aspect in product design, it is not thought about much in workplace design. The use of natural materials like wood or a rug brings in a warm, cozy feel. At the same time, artificial laminates bring in a rather clinical feel to a space. An experienced designer is able to establish a balance between complementary textures. Textures in the workplace are not only about furniture, but also about elements like artwork, greenery, carpets and the like.

Smell: Automatic air fresheners and scent disposal systems have made their way into workplaces too, smell being the most powerful of all senses. Aromatherapy is a well-established science and it has been seen that cinnamon, mint, lemon, orange and rosemary scents can enhance productivity. Pleasant odours not only enhance productivity, but also help improve memory. Such science, the application of which is relatively new for the workplace, has been used in the retail and hospitality sectors for many years. Carefully selected scents are pumped into the air in malls and in hotels, as they boost consumer spending and create a great brand experience.

Taste: Usually bundled with smell, taste may not be directly linked with productivity, but there can be indirect effects. What one eats at lunch can determine one's alertness levels thereafter. Too much of carbohydrates can lead to an afternoon sloth. Coffee helps in focus. Organizations that allow external contractors to run workplace cafeterias and restaurants can invite nutritionists to define the food menu. There is much benefit to be gained by including healthy eating as part of employee wellness programs.

Interior designers can step up to play an integrative role of designing on the basis of all five senses, which is in sync with the ethos of the organization. One size does not fit all; the ethos of a cellphone manufacturer will be very different from that of a food delivery app operator.

When it syncs, the space begins to act as an exoskeleton of the heart of the organization.

Distraction

In one of my early international business trips in the nineties, I landed in Hong Kong and made it to the hotel after taking the Airport Express train. As I arrived at my hotel, I was asked for my passport. I reached out to get my passport from an inner pocket in my backpack, and to my utter shock, it was not there. A chill went down my spine, as I looked in all the pockets of the backpack. Not finding it there, I checked my trouser pockets and the pockets of the suitcase I was carrying. The passport was nowhere to be found. In my calmest possible demeanor under the given circumstances, I told the receptionist that I seemed to have lost my passport. She listened patiently as I explained my predicament. She was kind enough to let me check-in on the basis of a photocopy of the passport that I had with me. She asked me to relax and think about where I might have dropped it. She assured me all possible help to recover the passport.

As I walked towards my room along a passage with floor-to-ceiling glass partitions overlooking Victoria Harbour, I failed to notice the beauty of the view. My mind was on overdrive with a hundred thoughts crossing it per second. Losing a passport in a foreign land is the worst nightmare one can have. My room had huge windows overlooking the bay and as I looked out, something in my mind told me to relax. I was physically tired after the long day at airports and in the air, and then this incident wore me out completely. I decided to take my mind off the problem at hand and thought about slipping into the luxurious bathtub that the room had. I drank some water. I then let the warm water fill the tub halfway and I slid in. From that position on the twenty something floor, I could see a bit of the massive expanse of water outside. As the warm water in the tub relaxed my muscles, I closed my eyes. It was therapeutic. I felt relaxed and went into a semi sleep state.

All of a sudden I woke up with a start. I knew where the passport was! I had last used it at the foreign exchange counter at the airport and when the cash was handed out to me, the passport was not handed over. I could visualize the entire scene like a flashback scene from a movie. It all came back to me in a flash, even though I was not thinking about my passport at all. I jumped out of the tub, put on some fresh clothes and rushed back to the reception. I narrated the turn of events to the receptionist. She quickly called up the 'lost and found' department at the airport and alerted them. She also organized a taxi to take me to the airport quickly. She told me to head straight to the 'lost and found' department at the airport as all lost goods are deposited at that department.

Once at the airport, I went straight to the lost and found department and lo and behold, my passport was there. The officer confirmed that it was found with the foreign exchange counter. He mentioned that the passport was handed over but I did not pick it up. I was quite sure it was not handed over. Anyway, it did not matter anymore. I had survived one of the worst nightmares one could have on foreign soil. I was so relieved.

Various experiments have been conducted to figure out if, when solving complex problems, it is better to remain focused on the problem or to distract oneself by doing something else? Does 'sleeping over it' really work?

Mark Twain is credited to have written his books while pacing around and dictating. Charles Dickens went for walks in the middle of his work to distract his mind, and the most brilliant of ideas came to him during walks. Mozart's best pieces came to him while he was on rides in horse drawn carriages. Research suggests that diverting the conscious mind unlocks one's creativity. When humans are faced with complex problems, the conscious mind goes on overdrive, trying to figure out a solution. However, the conscious mind has a limit on the amount of information it can process. So the mind simplifies the task by focusing on fewer elements of the problem at hand. When this happens, seemingly unimportant details are missed out, leading to half-baked solutions to problems. However, when the mind wanders, the sub conscious mind joins the dots between seemingly unrelated insights. Even if the conscious mind stops working, the sub conscious mind keeps working on it.

More importantly, the mind wanders to absorb a far wider array of insights. Out of this emerge some of the most creative thoughts. Remember waking up in the middle of the night with a solution to a problem that you were facing? Where were you the last time when a bright idea came to your mind? Chances are high that you may not have been sitting on your work desk, staring at a computer screen.

In a study with kids, two groups were given problems to solve. The kids in the first group had ADHD (Attention Deficit Hyperactivity Disorder) and the kids in the second group did not have ADHD. As expected, kids in the first group had trouble with problems, which required dedicated attention. However, this group outshone the other group when it came to problems, which required their creative and imagination abilities to be at the forefront. Similar studies done with adults have also shown that those with ADHD fare better than those without it, when it comes to creative tasks.

This indicates that the subconscious is actually better than the conscious in creative problem solving. When we distract ourselves and go for a walk in the middle of a complex problem solving exercise, we 'shut off' the conscious mind. However the subconscious is always 'on' in the background. It is particularly good at processing large amounts of seemingly unconnected information simultaneously.

In an experiment done at University College London, participants were asked to pick the odd one out on a screen covered with over 650 identical symbols. The odd one was a rotated version of the same symbol. Participants performed far better when they were given very little time to decide and had to rely on their subconscious, as compared to them getting more time. The subconscious has the ability to spot subtle visual differences. It also has the ability to perform complex calculations, often without the knowledge of the conscious.

The conscious mind is the rational part of the brain and often ends up vetoing the subconscious. Instinctive decisions in tests like these are more likely to be correct because the subconscious brain recognises a rotated version of the same object as different from the original, whereas the conscious brain sees the two objects as identical. For the conscious brain, an apple is still an apple whether rotated or not. So while the lower-level cognitive process spots the rotated image as the odd one out, the higher-level function overrides that decision and dismisses the rotated object because it is the same as all the other symbols. When subjects are given the time to engage their higher-level functions, their decisions were therefore more likely to be wrong.

At the workplace, when you quit thinking about the problem at hand, your subconscious mind doesn't quit working. This is the incubation stage. Thoughts keep colliding, and the subconscious mind keeps on making associations. Ideas come out of the blue. HR policies need to support workers' need to let go, to forget problems and do something else. Some of the most creative thoughts can emerge from such distraction

PLAY

At work, giving too much conscious attention to problems may backfire at times. One gets stuck as the conscious mind narrows thinking and limits cognitive resources to work with. This limits the choices for decision-making and one is often left with the feeling of a creative block.

The way to remove that block may be to walk away from the problem at hand and shut down the conscious mind for a bit. Some of the best ideas have come at such breaks from work; in the bathroom, during a walk in the park, during a ride on a train.

Imagine a pack of fifty dogs running on a road beside a forest. A dog in the middle will only see dogs all around it. However if it moves away from the pack and starts running at a distance from the pack, it will see the pack against a backdrop of the forest. The perspective changes. Decoupling from conscious attention is like changing the perspective. This gives the subconscious mind more insights to work upon and a solution emerges from the periphery.

Organizations have realized the importance of allowing workers to 'take a break', to exercise, to engage in sports and games, to be childlike.

When kids are asked to introduce themselves, they give some of the most fascinating introductions. Here is a sample:

> Hi, I am Jim. I like muddy puddles.
> Hi, I am Nikita. I love finger painting, and often use my sister's face as a canvas.
> Hi, I am Neil. I do boxing practice with the younger kids in the school bus.

There are two aspects to such introductions. Firstly it is unrestricted talk. With limited judging and censoring abilities, children speak with a free mind. They are naturally creative with their thoughts. Secondly there is always an element of play or exercise in such instructions. This indicates that creativity is interlinked with play and exercise.

As kids grow up, censorship comes in an effort to 'fit-in'. Parents and teachers in general teach the young ones what 'not to do' and how 'not to behave'. Children are taught 'A is for apple' instead of questioning what could be the different words that start with A. Children are taught that the sky is blue, as other hues of the sky are shunted out. This is akin to telling impressionable minds how 'not to be creative', and when such young minds enter the workplace, they have a lot of difficulty when forced to become creative, especially under the pressure of time. Young professionals who are given deadlines and pressurized to come up with solutions within a short time, often fail to come up with good solutions. This kind of forced linear thinking leaves no scope for the mind to look at the periphery for solutions. Far from solving problems, such candidates are often unable to define the problem accurately. Meanwhile, the self-introductions become less interesting as they reach college and quite boring when they start working. At the workplace, introductions begin to sound something like:

Hi, I am Jim. I am the Head of Marketing.
Hi, I am Nikita. I am in charge of Human Resources.
Hi, I am Neil. I am the Security Manager.

The childlike playfulness disappears. Putting adults in child-like mindsets help them open up their minds to opportunities, which lie in the periphery. All work and no play make Jack a dull boy. The social science is out there which imply that without opportunities to play any child will become depressed, withdrawn and antisocial. One can imagine what that means for an un-playful workplace.

So play is serious business. People are at their creative best during play and are able to overcome problems and meet challenges. Play is not predictable or repetitive. Researchers from the University of Pittsburgh & Carnegie Mellon have found that when people mentally prepare for a task and play with the available decision options, they activate the part of their brain which makes non-routine decisions.

Children and adults alike achieve the following when at play:

- Relate to other people
- Handle emotions
- Respond to challenges
- Cope with stressful experiences

Historically, play and fun has been seen as the opposite of work. As workplaces emerged as an extension of the shop floor, all that mattered was efficiency. Codified management theories and jargons developed around efficiency. Higher efficiency meant higher production. In this mindset, play and fun would appear to be adversely affecting efficiency and thereby diminish productivity. How one felt did not matter. However in the collaboration economy of today, where productivity depends on the quality of thinking, how an employee feels at work has come to the forefront.

Organizations have introduced elements in their workplaces, which allow workers to be playful. In smaller workplaces, interior designers are often asked to add basketball rings, table tennis tables, foosball tables, dart boards, mini golf, VR games, gym balls and the like. In larger campus type settings, one additionally comes across climbing walls, slides, trampolines, football, golf, jogging tracks, badminton and the likes.

However the mere introduction of elements, which allow workers to be playful, is not enough; it has to be supported by a management, which has a playful mindset. Management has to truly believe and support the fact that when an employee takes a break in the middle of his work for a quick game of table tennis, it will only boost his or her creativity at work and that he or she will be more productive. Being playful works only when workers can take play breaks without the fear of being looked down upon or worse, being castigated for it. In the absence of a change in management's attitude, the mere addition of games may actually backfire.

During the course of research for this book, amongst others, I spoke with a cousin of mine, who works with an organization that recently introduced several indoor games across the workplace. However when I asked her if she or her colleagues end up using these, the response was: 'rarely'. There was an apprehension that in the high-pressure environment of the organization, one would lag behind at work, adding to additional pressure, if one kept taking breaks in the middle of work. This is one of those high-pressure competitive organizations where deadlines mattered more than anything else. The management mindset had not changed in support of the top driven directive to add playful elements in the workplace.

Exercise

While writing this book and my previous books, at times, I have enjoyed a state of flow. In psychology, flow is the mental state of operation in which a person performing an activity is fully immersed in a feeling of energized focus, full involvement, and enjoyment in the process of the activity. In context of writing, it is the state when words flow easily.

But then, there have also been times when I get stuck. Words do not flow, and I cannot do much about it. These are those times when, however hard you think through a problem at hand, you cannot find a path to move forward. This not only happens when writing, but one is faced with that stuck feeling during day-to-day activities as well. It happens at home, it happens when one is working on a proposal submission with a tough deadline. When this happens, I usually get up and go for a brisk walk or for a jog, if the circumstances permit. Miraculously, in most instances, the block gets removed and things become crystal clear. It is like the lights turning on in a dark room. A study in the Journal of Experimental Psychology demonstrated that walking indoors and outdoors triggered a burst in creative thinking with the average creative output rising sixty percent when a person was walking.

In the collaboration economy of the twenty first century, the greatest human asset is the brain. Author of Brain Rules, John Medina, says that people who are physically active score better on cognitive tests than people living a sedentary lifestyle. In a clinical trial run by the Body-Brain Performance Institute in association with Swinburne's University and Brain Sciences Institute, there was a clear link established between physical fitness, brain function and reduced stress levels at work. An 'exercised' test group of participants showed a marked improvement in mood and cognition, with a four percent increase in overall brain function. When the brain is performing at full capacity, one can focus, concentrate, and make better decisions, all essential if creative and innovation are desired outcomes.

As workers spend most of their waking hours at work, organizations across the world are creating opportunities for workers to remain physically active. These include gyms at the workplace, walkways, jogging tracks and other active sports.

If I turn the clock back by about four decades, I am reminded of a time when I grew up in a much greener planet. As a child, I recall instances when we would come across snakes during hikes to the nearby hills. The instant reaction in spotting a snake would be to run. There was no time or knowledge to analyse if the snake was venomous or not.

If you could get on a time machine and turn the clock back by millions of years, you will see that our ancestors had the constant threat of becoming lunch for much larger predators. In front of such predators, man often had to choose between fighting the imminent danger or to run away from it. This is called the fight or flight response or the acute stress response, and was first described by Walter Bradford Cannon. According to him, there occurs a general discharge of the sympathetic nervous system, preparing one to fight or flee. All body systems shunt blood to the muscles and brain. It shunts blood away from the digestive system. During stress in the modern day context, one may sometimes feel like throwing up. That is because the blood gets diverted from the digestive system, leaving little time and resources to digest food.

Your breathing will increase so that you are taking in more oxygen for the muscles to work at their best. It will even make you breathe hard before contact. You may be so badly frightened by the situation that you may wet your pants or even defecate. And why would that help? It actually decreases extra body weight that you will have to carry if you decide to run away. Every little bit may make the difference. Your adrenalin levels will rise. This is the reason behind the jittery feeling that you may get. Your pupils will get larger as your brain tries to see as much as possible.

The modern day equivalent of predators hiding in the grasslands and jumping at you could be someone hiding in a dark room and shouting, "Boo!" as you enter. Your body will yell at you to "run or fight!"; else you die. Although today's workers do not have too many predators waiting at street corners, they are faced with stress from a barrage of emails, deadlines, phone calls and bosses. On top of that, there is way too much information being fed onto one's lives, thanks to social networking, internet, television and instant messaging. These ensure that one is bombarded with a lot of bad news during the day. The combination of these along with work related pressure, leads to acute stress. Our bodies are designed to respond with a physiological response when under stress. Without it, one runs the risk of suffering from high anxiety and depression.

When one exercises, the mood gets a high due to the release of endorphins in the bloodstream. The increased blood flow to the brain sharpens one's awareness. The brain also gets ready to absorb and process more information. Exercise enhances your body's ability to transfer glucose and oxygen throughout your brain and body, thus increasing your energy level.

I was once part of a leadership development program for workers of a client organization. Although I was called in for a half-day workshop session, I got the opportunity to spend some quality time with participants beyond my assigned time. Participants were made to start the day early with various forms of exercise like yoga, walking and strength training. After a few days of 'working out' early, the participants were clearly more focused and engaged; and they did not suffer from the post lunch sloth. Our client mentioned that this group of participants could retain more concepts compared to participants in similar programs in the past, which had not included the early morning exercise regime. Exercise improves alertness and focus. It does ultimately improve job performance.

Fully equipped gyms are increasingly being made part of new workplaces. Where space is a constraint to do this, workers are given gym memberships in the neighbourhood. In the campuses of Infosys in India, Apple Park and Googleplex in California, workers are encouraged to cycle from one department to another or simply to 'go cycling' every once in a while. Good quality wireless headphones also enable workers to participate in conference calls while taking a stroll in the campus garden.

The importance of design, from a holistic perspective, cannot be understated. In times when space is a mix of the physical and digital, it is no more about styling. Design influences what we think, the way we feel and the decisions we make. It is crucial for management to take cognizance of this reality and look at this new idea of space as an extension of the organization's ethos. This new space is like the exoskeleton of what the heart of the organization is; both need to sync and work in harmony to achieve a state of flow in business.

CREATIVITY

Steve Wozniak, co-founder of Apple, during a visit to India in 2018, said this about India "'Success in India is based on studying, having a job...where's the creativity?" He elaborated thus: "The culture here is one of success based upon academic excellence, studying, learning, practicing and having a good job and a great life. The creativity gets left out when your behaviour is too predictable and structured, everyone is similar." This is a rather sad reality, especially about the globally renowned Indian tech industry. Despite a leadership legacy spanning more than two decades, the industry has largely remained focused on services and has failed to offer to the world any path-breaking product.

Creativity does not emerge out of a structured, linear approach to work and life. This safe path makes life predictable and creativity is left on the wayside. There is no secret formula for creativity. Each has their own way. When you ask the so-called creative geniuses what makes them creative, they usually do not seem to know or have a common answer. However, one aspect stands out. Most creative geniuses appear to be non-structured in their efforts. They wander, daydream, try and fail a lot at what they do, and this leads them to a sense of 'purposeful accident', out of which emerges a truly innovative idea.

They look around, tinker with various things, and are able to connect the dots, by drawing inspiration from seemingly unrelated aspects of life. When one looks outside the realm of what is connected, one is not mentally constrained by the existing, 'known' solutions to the problem at hand. This often tends to be a potential source of radical innovation. The greater the distance between the problem and the analogous field, the greater is the novelty of the emerging solution.

So looking around makes business sense. Creative geniuses are not constrained by the assumed limitations and mental schemas of their own professional world. These are the guys, who do not remain fixated to their laptop screens, going through the latest sales numbers on a flight, but chatting away with the guy on the next seat. These are those who read unrelated stuff and not bury themselves in tomes containing articles around their own professional work. The more one looks around, the more mental stimuli the brain gets access to.

The trouble with most workplaces is that workers are subjected to the same information and professional sphere of things day after day. Meetings, calls, emails and presentations that fill up a worker's day only accentuate the rigidity of being stuck within a structured approach, similar to Steve Wozniak's view of the Indian culture of good education followed by a good job, which is then followed by a good car and a good house. A safe and predictable approach rarely allows any creativity to occur.

Slowly a small group of forward thinking organizations are trying to break through this mental rut and encouraging their workers to be more explorative. Building workplaces, which allow the mind to adopt an explorative bent, helps. However this needs to be supported by a mindset change from top down. Workers are being encouraged and in rare cases even sponsored to spend a portion of their time pursuing their own passion. Libraries, music rooms, yoga rooms, multipurpose rooms which morph into employee art galleries and dance rooms are slowly but surely becoming a part of design briefs for interior designers.

SLEEPING AT WORK

According to Vitalityhealth/Rand Eurpor, 29.6% of workers sleep less than seven hours per night and lose an equivalent of 4.7 productive days per year.

A study lead by Ronald Kessler, Ph.D., a psychiatric epidemiologist at Harvard Medical School, in Boston says that insomnia costs U.S. $63 billion annually in lost productivity. About one-third of all U.S. adults experience difficulties with nighttime sleep, and an estimated fifty to seventy million people complain of associated daytime impairment, the study notes.

On the other side of the globe, the scene is not very different in India. Nearly 56 per cent of corporate workers sleep less than 6 hours in a day due to high stress levels that arise out of tough targets set by employers, according to an ASSOCHAM Healthcare Committee report in 2018.

For pilots, drivers or firefighters, lack of sleep can potentially lead to errors, leading to loss of life. The Federal Aviation Administration in the USA, require that pilots get at least ten hours of rest between shifts. Eight of those hours must involve uninterrupted sleep. Pilots are limited to flying eight or nine hours, depending on the start times. They must also have thirty consecutive hours of rest each week.

Since the link between lack of sleep amongst regular office-goers and accidents are not as apparent as in the case of drivers and pilots, there appears to be no sleep protocols at the workplace.

The CEO and MD of a multinational corporation died, while on a jog at the age of 42, in Mumbai, India. He was very active in sports, was a fitness freak and a marathon runner. In an interview with a television channel he had mentioned that he used to make do with 4-5 hours of sleep and admitted that he would love to get more sleep. This is how bad, lack of sleep can get at the workplace.

In general, one may have trouble concentrating, working, making decisions, remembering things, and being one's best selves, due to lack of adequate sleep. One can get irritable and unpleasant to be around. But the problem is more serious than just being in a bad mood.

Stress, diabetes, high blood pressure and other health complications pile up when one does not get adequate sleep. Without a holistic employee wellness program, such fallouts may remain outside the lenses of management. Organizations, till recently, have continued to ignore sleep wellness as part of employee wellness, and have focused on diet, weight, exercise and smoking cessation. However what is slowly bringing the importance of sleep into the forefront is that productivity dips at the workplace when one does not get enough sleep. Concentration and quality of thinking slows down when the body is not rested. This matters a lot in the collaboration economy where the quality of thinking determines productivity. Moreover, the ability to be empathetic to colleagues diminishes when the body is not rested. This impacts interpersonal relationships and teamwork at the workplace.

So even though, lack of sleep may not have the on-the-surface potential to kill for the white collared worker like in the case of the pilot, it can have drastic indirect impact. Someone working in finance may end up making a bad decision because they are not well rested, and that leads to a company failing or an agreement failing and many people losing their jobs.

Progressive organizations are doing their bit to help workers overcome their stigma over sleeping at work, as they realize that sleeping on the job actually makes business sense. Sleeping rooms and sleeping pods are slowly getting introduced within the workplace as organizations from cross industry segments like Google, Cisco, PwC, KPMG and White & Case introduce their workers to sleeping at work.

Futuristic looking sleeping pods are infused with digital technology, allowing workers to take a short nap. The pods help cut off the ambient light and the worker is woken up before one goes into deep sleep. One wakes up feeling recharged and ready to go for a few more hours of productive work.

SWITCHING OFF

In 2013, I wrote 'Smart Phones, Dumb People?', my first book. This was a general commentary on how smart digital technology is affecting human behavior. Since 2013, digital technology has made quantum leaps and is much more entrenched in our personal and professional lives. Almost everyone at a Starbucks is either looking at their cellphones or onto their laptop screens, prompting the question if it is a coffee shop anymore. The guy who is having a coffee without a gadget in his hand is the one who stands out, almost like a zombie. What is wrong with him?

Studies indicate that:

- 84% of cellphone users claim they could not go a single day without their device.
- 67% of cellphone owners check their phone for messages, alerts, or calls — even when they don't notice their phone ringing or vibrating.
- Mobile device owners check their devices every 6.5 minutes.
- 88% of U.S. consumers use mobile devices as a second screen even while watching television.
- Almost half of cellphone owners have slept with their phone next to their bed because they wanted to make sure they didn't miss any calls.

'Cellphone checking' is the new yawn because of its contagious nature. What does it mean for the workplace? The average worker spends a full day of their workweek doing things other than, well, work.

A survey found that the average office worker spends 56 minutes per day using their cellphone at work for non-work activity. That works out to just under five hours per week of non-productive work on phones. Personal email and social media made up the majority of the wasted time, with sports sites, mobile gaming, and shopping placed a distant third, fourth and fifth place.

At the workplace, one does not want to miss out on what is happening outside of work, and outside the workplace there is an unspoken need to be available round the clock. Cellphones allow us to do this. This is leaving no time for the brain to recover.

It is about time that workers are reminded that technology has a switch off button. That button was given so that one can switch off at times. In recent times, I have come across organizations that have tweaked their email servers to stop them from transmitting emails after office hours and during weekends. Others have programmed the server to delete emails when workers are on vacation. Some organizations have gone an extra mile and made vacationing mandatory for workers.

As workers juggle between the burrow holes of digital space and the physical space, the new blended workplace ought to allow opportunities for workers to disconnect. Life is still about flesh and blood. It is about eye contact and the five senses, and hence the need to look up from the screens.

SECTION 3: How do we do it?

Given my educational background in design, I am, at times, pulled into discourses around creativity and about innovation. The word innovation has gained tremendous currency over the last ten years, thanks largely to the proliferation of digital technology and a general belief that digital technology can solve, well, nearly all problems that face the world. The world of business management, which loves codified processes, has developed its own set of dos and don'ts on how to crack innovation. One such evolution is the design thinking methodology.

This is not a design book but a book on business management. Across my nearly three decades of association with the world of design and management, I have seen design take two impactful meanings. Firstly, design as styling. Years back, it was believed that design can be the great differentiator, especially in product development. Customers will buy your products if you are distinctly different by way of design. This is only partially true today, as no organization will release a product in the market if it is not well designed. Everyone is doing it.

Secondly, the evolution of design thinking as another codified management process, which revolves around user centricity. If product developers can understand the end user of a product at a basic, human level and get to know their true aspirations, one can surprise end users with truly innovative products, which were not expected. The end users will accept such products as it taps onto their unmet aspirations.

I have had the opportunity to interact closely with clients who have used design-thinking principles. Design thinking works, and quite well, until your competitor also begins to adopt design-thinking principles. Then one begins to lose the strategic advantage. This codification of design thinking into a management process, defeats the very basic principle of design; i.e. to differentiate. The quick proliferation of design thinking experts, trainers and organizations adopting the method, makes me wonder if this is going the TQM (Total Quality Management) way. There was a time, when processes like Six Sigma were seen as a differentiator. Today quality is a given. Customers simply do not accept products, which do not embody quality.

So where does one go from here? Is technology the one true sustainable differentiator?

In the twenty first century, digital technology has led to the disruption of several business structures and helped in the birth of new structures. Uber, AirB&B and Facebook have respectively changed the existing structures of the transportation industry, travel industry and human behavior itself. When the timing and context is right, technology has the ability to affect tectonic shifts. When combined with an understanding of user needs, using design-thinking principles, a potent combination emerges. The only possible limitation in this combination is that a future imagined on past and current human expectations is not exactly reflective of what will work in the future. One needs to step back a little from this perspective and take a macro view.

An artist often steps back from his canvas to look at it from a distance. With a perspective change, the art looks different. Those pursuing innovation are like artists. They need to step back once in a while, step back from codified processes and approach innovation with a visionary approach. When it comes to business success, organizations will always find themselves doing a balancing act between past legacy, current success and the future. When doing crystal ball gazing, stepping back from codified process that worked in the past or working in the present, will help innovation teams see a new vision. This relates to new products and new services, which will be bought by customers. This requires the product developers and the innovation specialists to think and behave differently when it comes to future products and services. They need to look for new meanings behind things that people do.

Incremental innovation gives us products with new features, functions and superior performance. However customers do not buy into product features and functions but into meanings. A loyal iPhone customer will buy a new iPhone model, despite other products in the market with far more features and lower price. This is because the iPhone means something to him. Similarly a visit to the neighbourhood Starbucks is not anymore about the coffee. You usually buy the coffee to pay for the time spent at Starbucks doing something else.

Without the 'need' to go to a workplace, thanks to technology, the aspirations of the millennials from a workplace is drastically different from those of the previous generations. The meaning of work and the workplace is very different for the millennials as compared to previous generations

When it comes to innovation from the standpoint of changing the meaning of things for customers, it needs to start at home. The outlook of the organization and its people has to change first. This book is about changing that outlook; about changing the heart of the organization. The workplace is the external manifestation of that change of heart. It makes sense to use the workplace as the starting point of innovation.

HAPPINESS

I am the father of two young daughters who have grown up in a consumerist society. I learnt a few lessons on happiness as my elder daughter was growing up, which helped me with daughter number two. As new parents, my wife and I used to give one relatively expensive gift on our elder daughter's birthday. This is one day that she began to eagerly look forward to, because of the gift from us. Of course there would be additional gifts from friends and fun filled activities throughout the day. However we soon realized that the joy of acquiring something new disappeared rather fast. The excitement of owning a new shiny pink bicycle disappeared within less than a month of cycling on it.

Soon we realized that whether it was a bicycle or a chocolate bar, she would return to her happiness equilibrium sooner or later. Happiness seems to have a base level. So it made more sense to giver her smaller, less expensive things at frequent intervals, rather than one big thing annually. This would help sustain her level of happiness at a certain high for most of the time. This was also lighter on the pocket. But then, hey, they are our daughters and not lab rats, so we did not really conduct this as a lab experiment. A look at psychology does confirm this hypothesis: humans return to their happiness equilibrium within a certain period of time.

This is also true about sadness. So, if one is shocked by an unexpected event, over a period of time, he or she will return to equilibrium. Twenty-four hour news channels play on this, and tend to rely on breaking news all the time. However shocking a new piece of news is in the beginning, viewers find it less and less shocking over time. In the absence of new shocking news, television channels rely on sensationalization to titillate viewers.

Today's urban dwellers are well informed about what is going on around them and around the world. The average office goer, driven by FOMO (fear of missing out) thrives on the novelty of things and experiences. They want to experience something new all the time, and often end up buying things that they do not need, for that insatiable desire to consume something new.

Such a desire to experience something new all the time spells out in the workplace as well. The initial high of getting a new job involves meeting new people, getting a higher pay, experiencing a new workplace. But as novelty wears out, one yearns for something new. So it is not surprising to find workers starting to look for new jobs within months of joining a new job, for no apparent problem at the workplace. The same yearning for novelty leads people to keep on changing cars and other material possessions like cellphones every now and then.

At the blended workplace of the physical and the digital, it has become pertinent for HR to facilitate workers to experience something new every now and then. Humans, by nature, have a deeply curious nature. This embedded curiosity leads humans to do unproductive things like reading about people one will never meet, learning topics one will never have use for. People just love to know the answers to things, even if there's no obvious benefit.

Conventionally HR has looked at staff reviews as an annual review to figure out 'what they want'. In a world of twenty-four hours news channels, it is about time to relook at such reviews as an annual feature. The millennial generation does not have the patience to wait for the annual review and the possible salary hike; they want constant feedback about their performance. If something is not working out, they would want to try something 'new'. So, while an annual bonus is welcome and seen mostly as a reward for hard work, what works much better are monthly or quarterly reviews, along with feedback and encouragement about one's work.

A monthly outing with colleagues works much better than an annual jaunt and a bonus. It helps keep interpersonal relationships healthy and team spirit alive. Secondly, such experiences go way further than monetary benefits in strengthening the engagement of workers to an organization. That is because, team based activities like a game or a picnic is enjoyed in the company of other humans. This raises the happiness level and sustains it. A monetary dole-out is enjoyed in one's privacy, leading to a quicker fall back to the happiness equilibrium. A fun weekend spent with colleagues is remembered for years to come, and strengthens employee engagement; however an annual bonus does relatively little to build sustained engagement.

Closer home, at the workplace, building spaces, which allow a variety of experiences to be played out regularly, is good practice. A games room can be the venue for monthly inter-departmental competitions. A cafeteria, which allows re-configuration, can be themed for various themed get-togethers. Irrespective of the size of the workplace, if there is an attitudinal change to increase the happiness quotient from the top, it will flow down to affect all.

Similar to my experience with my daughters, from an organization standpoint, it is likely to cost much less to give frequent smaller doses of happiness than a big fat dose at the end of the year. Towards this, co-working spaces are leading the trend of building workplaces that allow occupants to ride the novelty wave and sustain it.

CO-WORKING SPACES

A lot of work happens in coffee shops, restaurants and airports today. I have been to innovative eateries that have introduced membership packages, allowing members to work with their laptops from such places. Membership includes wifi, power sockets and a place to sit as basics and additional services like printing that can be bought. Members can collect royalty points and utilize such points and cash for either food or other services. Such eateries are tapping on to the shift to a 'pay-per-use' state of mind by a generation that prefers a cab-hailing app like Uber, to car ownership, that prefers streaming services from Netflix to traditional television. Pay-per-use is gaining popularity due to the flexibility it offers, the wide choice of services, different rates of pay and of course pay per use basis. A co-working space is the bridge between a coffee shop that offers free wifi and the conventional workplace.

Ever since iDream started consulting multinational corporations on using space as a starting point of innovation, we have been occasionally asked to conduct workshops for decision makers, around the topic. Besides the regular workshops at the workplaces of client organizations, I have had the opportunity to conduct some of these familiarization workshops within the vibrant environments of co-working spaces.

A co-working space is a shared workplace where one can rent out workstations, meeting rooms, offices and other facilities. One shares the workplace with other organizations and with other entrepreneurs. One has the choice of starting small, renting a single workstation on hourly, daily or weekly basis. An organization can also rent hundreds of workstations on annual basis. The flexibility of choosing the type of space, the duration flexibility and the relatively low cost for the space, has made co-working spaces very popular. What began as something for startups has caught the fancy of large organizations as well. Larger co-working operators are targeting multinational corporations with annual contracts for hundreds of workstations. As this happens, the dynamics of the real estate and fit-out industries change; client organizations benefitting from the lack of investment into fit-outs and complex rental agreements. In a matter of five years or so, the number of co-working spaces has grown fast, mushrooming across major urban centres in the world.

Besides the flexibility of time and space, co-working spaces offer two great benefits. Firstly, most co-working spaces are designed as workplaces where occupants get the opportunity to explore various types of settings. Add to this the blended nature of such spaces where free wifi and tools like videoconferencing consoles allow occupants to seamlessly transit the physical and the digital realms. Occupants can seat themselves at different types of workstations, offices, beanbags, telephone booths, sofas, and cafeterias as they transit between the two realms. Not only does this allow a high degree of mental stimulation, enabling creative thoughts, but it also allows occupants to meet and interact with co-occupants who come from a variety of backgrounds. An app developer may be sitting next to an architect who may be sitting next to a social media professional. This proliferates a lab kind of setting where casual interactions and water cooler moments are likely to encourage creativity and ideation.

Secondly, the novelty of something new happening is usually sustained longer in well designed co-working spaces, when compared with dedicated workplaces for a single organization. Occupants keep on meeting new people all the time, working on un-heard of things. Moreover, most co-working operators keep on organizing weekly or monthly events to keep the novelty factor high. Workshops, talks, stand-up comedy, beer weekends, pizza days are common in the vibrant co-working spaces. Such mental stimulation keeps occupants engaged towards the co-working community.

In an always-connected world, the co-working spaces are like the physical manifestation of online social networking sites. A co-working space allows one to work in isolation when required, to collaborate when required, to relax and recharge when required. Moreover they are popular because they culturally fit-in to the 'pay-per-use' approach towards services that the current generation is good at. The design of co-working spaces is representative of the unspoken demands of the new-age worker, as I have captured in the previous pages. Blended workplaces of the future are poised to take this direction.

During the summer of 2014, towards the end of my time at Oxford University, England, I chanced upon a coffee house there, called the Grand Cafe. It claims to be the first coffee house in England, established in 1650. I think it was one of the first forms of co-working spaces in England. The coffee houses of the 17th and 18th century were the engines of creation that helped drive the Enlightenment – the intellectual movement of the time that emphasized reason and individualism over tradition. Men visited these coffee shops to have a conversation, catch up with the gossip, get the latest news and connect. It was the internet of the time. One could gain entry by buying a coffee for one penny. So much of ideation and opinions flowed from these coffee houses that they came to be known as penny universities.

Centuries later, Starbucks and their ilk gave a contemporary new meaning to coffee houses, by offering the internet and coffee. To that extent, the forward integration of modern day coffee houses in the form of co-working spaces, are the new penny universities. Modern day spaces that fuel ideation.

A space that allows ideas to knock against each other, leading to possible Eureka moments is the kind of space that will welcome innovation. The new workplace can be imagined as a university campus, which is a web of blended spaces. A university campus has spaces for collaboration, spaces for solitude, spaces for learning, spaces for focused study, spaces for exercise & play and spaces for rest. A workplace that reflects such a setting will become the starting point of innovation.

QUESTIONS TO ASK

The new workplace is one where the physical and the digital merge. This is not something futuristic, but this is how we conduct our personal and professional lives today and how workplaces are being imagined. This blended space allows one to seamlessly move from a physical realm to a digital realm and vice versa.

One can see early examples like the Telepresence suite by Cisco, first introduced in 2006. It is a combination of physical and digital products designed to link two physically separated rooms so that they resemble a single room. The two rooms could be in two different continents. We were involved in setting up such a room in Bangalore in those early years, and it required a very high degree of precision. The results were amazing. The pictures were amazingly clear and when people on the other side spoke, it seemed as if the sound was coming from their mouths. It is so real that you may accidentally try to shake hands with the person on the other side or pass on papers.

Ever since then, virtual reality has made much progress. We are staring at a not-so-distant future where virtual reality will enable us to conduct meetings with holographic, realistic versions of colleagues in other parts of the world. This will further reduce the need to travel for meetings. Such a reality, where human productivity is augmented by digital technology, requires one to change one's approach at setting up new workplaces.

The technology available today itself has obliterated the need to 'go to work', leave alone what will happen in ten years to come. This, when combined with the dying breed of white collared workers who go to work for a promotion and the hope of a higher salary, requires a radical change in the questions asked when setting up new workplaces.

The conventional linear approach of setting up the workplace has been rather structured. The facilities department works with interior designers and engineering consultants to design the workplace. Contractors build the workplace. The HR department defines the way workers are expected to work from the workplace; IT department plugs in the technology to get the work done. And so on and so forth; each department working with their set of vendors independently, without much coordination between them.

Design briefs to interior designers include statements like:

- Making the new workplace cheerful
- Making the new workplace colourful
- An open and transparent workplace

The trouble with this linear approach is that when a statement like open and transparent workplace is doled out, the designer will do down the path of identifying all components which makes a workplace transparent and open. The predictable result is to create a workplace that is a judicious mix of all these components. The exploration while conceptualizing the workplace remains limited to the interior designer and his or her network, the facilities department and around the topic of openness.

The challenge for the organization is to step back a little, and relook at the question. Should the question be about how to make a better workplace (incremental innovation) or about finding a new meaning for workers to want to come to work? Organizations need to find a new meaning for workers to report to work; else they face the risk of people not coming to work. Like water finding the path of least resistance, humans are wired to take the path of least resistance. That is why people change jobs instead of struggling with promotion. That is why customers do not visit offline stores if an online order fulfills their needs. That is why people will stop going to work if they can fulfill their desires without going.

Like the diminishing queues of people collecting cash at teller counters of banks, people have stopped buying air-tickets from airline counters, thanks to the ease of doing it online. We worked closely with Singapore Airlines in 2018 as they faced the problem of unproductive, expensive real estate. Technology reduced human interaction drastically, requiring the airline to adopt a new real estate strategy in line with the new reality. So, if people do not need to go, they will not go, unless a new meaning is found. When it comes to workplaces, the question needs to change from "How do we build a cheerful workplace?" to something like: "How do we motivate people to come to work?" This broad question needs to be fine-tuned in line with the organization's vision of the future.

When such questions are asked, the ecosystem of influencers who can contribute to find the answers, changes. The web is widened and not limited to interior designers any more. The social angle comes in, so does human psychology. What are the social changes, which affect the meaning of work in the collaboration economy? What are the psychological aspects to the issue? The collaborators required to set-up the new workplace change to embrace a wide range of professionals.

When the question changes to motivation for coming to work, the subject gets broadened from a workplace to motivation and life. All of a sudden, you begin to see the existence of parallel discourses around motivation. Then, by saying people, a human angle comes in. The study of human aspirations comes into play. You soon begin to realize that seemingly disconnected professionals are conducting research around the general topic of human motivation. There is much to learn from such parallel research, which can go a long way in contributing to building the new workplace. These other professionals, outside of your organization's four walls, are usually happy to share their research, thoughts and contribute to the broader discourse.

In my work with corporate organizations, I have seen the expectation from an interior designer change rather drastically over the last two decades. In the twentieth century, the interior designer's role was largely limited to designing the interior space of a new workplace. Over time, expectations changed and designers were expected to take additional responsibility of building services like electrical and air-conditioning. Then, as IT became the backbone of organizations, interior designers were expected to take comprehensive design roles and coordinate with other consultants to include topics like data cabling, server racks, security systems, etc. Today, an interior designer who specializes in workplace design is expected to be in sync with and be knowledgeable about the latest digital technology, along with knowledge about latest trends in workplace design and building services. Similarly, other stakeholders involved in setting up new workplaces like contractors, hardware manufacturers and project managers are expected to step out of their comfort zone, be aware about the latest trends in workplaces and at times even be responsible for delivering products and services that are sub-contracted and not directly linked with their line of work. As roles expand, it is critical for client organizations to take a step back and look at the larger picture.

By stepping back to look at it from a broader angle in context of new meaning of work, workers and the workplace, one realizes that one is not alone in the efforts to understand changes in society, culture and technology and its impact on work, the worker and the workplace. Management consulting firms do considerable research, furniture and fixture manufacturers do continuous studies, and computer manufacturers spend millions of dollars in understanding the changing needs of the white collared worker. IT firms are deep into research in this area and so are university professors and students. Most of them are trying to answer the same question; how the new-age worker finds new meaning in work and the workplace. Secondly, they also play a key role in influencing people's meanings, desires and aspirations. Organizations, by tapping onto such influencers' knowledge, can be at the forefront of driving innovation from the ground up, from within their organization, by relooking at the changing nature of work, workers and the workplace.

WHO ARE THESE INFLUENCERS?

So while setting up the new workplace, who are these influencers? There are two broad factors that are influencing massive change in people's lives in the twenty first century; firstly technology and secondly social changes. Influencers can thus be broadly classified into two categories: the technology influencers and the social influencers.

Technology influencers

Technology has had the most profound influence in changing the way we live in the twenty first century. Influencers include those who lead technical innovations, discoveries and new products & services. By doing this, they change the meaning behind doing certain things. Notable technology influencers include:

Educational institutions: An enormous amount of technology related research and development takes place in educational institutions. Design and engineering institutes often lead this by way of annual research projects. Several progressive institutes often work, under the guidance of learned professors, on research projects for corporate organizations. Not all of these are illusionary in nature, with the hope of finding ready-to-use solutions. Forward thinking organizations have found merit in collaborating closely with like-minded institutions to co-create solutions through focused research. This often involves sharing of resources like labs, co-organising public discourses and workshops on the given topic. Successful projects go the extra mile to address the interactions between technology and social change.

Suppliers: Forward looking suppliers like furniture manufacturers, carpet manufacturers, light fitting manufactures often conduct deep research on productivity at the workplace, ergonomics, material science and even information technology & digital technology. Some global players even delve into the realm of the connection between feeling good and productivity at the workplace, incorporating such insights into product development. Leading furniture manufacturers have begun incorporating digital elements into furniture, as they try to make the experience of transiting from the digital to the physical realm seamless. There is much to gain from such research findings, that most suppliers are happy to share with client organizations.

Digital technology suppliers: Technology is all over the place in the new workplace. In the blended workplace, there are suppliers who augment the physical space by developing and supplying smart building components. Then there are those that augment the digital space with the research and development around products and services. As human effort is reduced by the infusion of technology advancement at the workplace, much effort is spent in understanding the impact of this on human behavior. The insights from such observation are sent back to the drawing table for incremental innovation on existing products as well as breakthrough innovation around new products. Client organizations can leverage much from such learnings; all they need to do is ask and most suppliers are happy to work closely with client organizations to arrive at fresh insights around the man vs. machine debate, and the massive changes brought on by augmented reality.

Social influencers

These are people and organizations that study and influence social changes, on how humans in general are affected by social disruptions around them and how new popular culture evolves. A few examples are:

Sociologists: In Section 2, I have written about the evolution of human behavior and how this influences certain behavior. Understanding such evolution is very helpful for HR professionals to understand the present day worker's behavior and their aspirations. There are professional agencies that conduct social science experiments, and analyze society and culture. Interaction with such influencers helps to understand social science phenomena that influence work, workers and the workplace. Besides ongoing research on social science and anthropology, a whole lot of existing data, which proves certain hypothesis about the modern workplace, needs to be tapped onto.

Designers: In conventional thinking, interior designers are given the overall responsibility to conceptualise the new workplace. Client managers, supported by a design brief, give designers a generic understanding of the end users. This is a rather narrow approach, as designers are trained to do space planning and styling. Designers play a pivotal role and can play the role of the coordinator and tap into the knowledge bank of other co-influencers, if given that briefing. However they miss doing this, due to a lack of a 'step away' approach from client organizations and also due to time constraints. Time constraints are a result of following convention, which is structured with boundaries of time, budgets and outlook. However, most experienced designers are well exposed to global trends in workplace design. Such knowhow needs to be tapped onto and superimposed with other learnings about the changing nature of work and workers.

Media: There are multiple dialogues in traditional and social media around changing cultural norms and the changing nature of work, workers and workplaces. These people observe social changes, popular culture and the influence on human behavior, at home and at work. Given the wide proliferation of social media in the last decade, a lot of the noise floating around is either repeated points or useless noise. In the middle of this, one occasionally comes across forward thinking discourses; organizations can tap into them and sync such thinking with the emerging meaning and motivation for workers to go to the workplace.

Architects: Architects are trained to take a macro, socio-cultural view of projects as the life of most buildings usually outlasts the current vision of client organizations. Secondly they look at a project through the lenses of the surrounding language of structures, as fitment becomes important in the local context, partly constrained by regulations. This macro outlook is very helpful in developing the collective discourse.

Real Estate Consultants: Consultants that help organizations broker new commercial property are usually clued in to the latest trends and expectations around work, workers and workplaces. Well-informed ones also keep track of policy changes, and can bring in a much needed macro perspective.

Workers: Workers are the users, the beneficiaries. In design thinking, the end users take centre stage and solutions emerge on the basis of an understanding of their unmet needs at a human level. This is done through observation, securing insights from such insights, and then discovering opportunities, followed by ideas and finally solutions. We have used tried and tested techniques to co-create solutions with users for several client organizations. However simply following this codified methodology will be doing a disservice to them, as workers are not mere receivers. They can contribute to the greater good and the broader understanding of the changing nature of work and the workplace. At times, workers can participate in deep research as part of following the design thinking principles and contribute to groundbreaking innovation by way of completely new insights into the changing nature of work itself.

The list above is generic in nature. Depending on the nature of the organization's work, other influencers may be added. The ability to tap onto this collective research laboratory will help organizations understand how one can give new meaning to work, workers and the workplace; and the inspiration thereof.

The challenge beyond the identification of the influencers, is:

- Firstly to carefully observe the ongoing discourses
- Secondly to interpret it in the context of the organization's vision and
- Thirdly to incorporate it within the subject organization.

This method of stepping back and taking a broader perspective, identifying and listening to influencers and finally to learn from such influencers and incorporate it within the organization's context of work, workers and workplace can be easily extended to the organization's vision of future products and services. In such a case, one needs to step back a little from being too user focused; observing and interpreting influencers to develop a new vision for future products and services. When product development and the organization's vision for the future is in sync with the new meaning of work, workers and the workplace, each component in the organization's DNA will deliver on their value proposition.

AN INTEGRATIVE PROCESS

Interior designers are trained to work magic inside the four walls of a building. Architects, on the other hand, are trained to design the building itself. Increasingly one finds a large number of Architects trying their hand at workplace interiors too. Architects, especially some of the established ones, carry a reputation of not listening to their clients and pushing their own vision. Fact of the matter is that Architects are never trained to listen to clients. As they have to design buildings, which will mostly, outlast the lives and current vision of clients, they usually step back a little from the current vision and take a wider view in context of history of time. Secondly, Architects carry the additional responsibility of coming up with something, which fits into the context of the general landscape.

On the other hand, interior designers are trained to listen in to the current needs and desires of clients, as interior fit-outs tend to have a shelf-life which is in sync with the current vision of client organizations, usually in the five-to-ten years range. It is the joint responsibility of client organizations and interior designers to bring about flexibility in a project such that designers can listen to the needs and desires of the end users as well. Listening to a client is not the same as listening to the end user; the former tends to be management and the latter the workers. A look through a micro lens is key to fulfilling unmet aspirations of end users.

At a pivotal level, client organizations need to play the role of an artist, such that one does not get stuck at the micro level, and the occasional stepping back takes place. The organization needs to play an integrative role with the various influencers and immerse itself deeply. The quality of thinking is directly proportional to the quality of integration amongst the various influencers. The big question here is how does one identify these influencers?

While setting up new workplaces or for any new initiative in organizations, there is a general belief that hiring a famous or experienced player in the subject domain is the solution. This works well for projects where the need is to make incremental improvements. In such cases, given the 'past' experience, the innovation focus is based on the past and current understanding of users' needs and aspirations. However in cases where one needs to think about shaping the future, relying on past experience is not likely to work.

This book is based on the premise that humans do not need to 'go to work' anymore. We are trying to figure out ways in which we can keep the workplace relevant and use that as a starting point of innovation itself. This requires a radical change of meaning to go to work. To find influencers who can contribute to this radical change, one needs to look outside the structure of competitions to hire organizations on the basis of past success. Competitions can bring in tons of great 'free' ideas, however it is not possible for anyone to propose ideas that will work, in context of the radical change, without them being part of the integrated collective. Do not hire ideas, but hire ideators.

A radical change of meaning calls for a client organization to immerse themselves completely to be part of the silent buzz. There are radical thinkers out there, and such thinkers are usually not part of competitions.

Looking for influencers in context

While this book talks broadly about finding new meaning for coming to work, an organization will need to go deep to arrive at a more precise meaning, which is aligned with its vision for the future. Once that is done, one needs to look for influencers who are conducting research around that. Let us say that the new meaning involves motivation as a key driver. So, when it comes to motivation, besides the usual suspects as listed before, one can even explore researchers, professors, speakers who study motivation itself. One can explore product manufacturers that specialize in motivational products.

One needs to ask how do such influencers give new meaning to things under the same context of motivation. This is important to understand because radical change comes from elements that were previously non-existent in a given environment.

For example, the original user context of the beanbag in the sixties and the seventies, is not different from the context of millennial workers. The target user of the first beanbags was the lax, hippie community and their non-conformist household, in an era characterized by apartment sharing and student demonstrations. Fast-forward to the millennial generation, and one can draw several similarities between the life context of two generations separated by nearly fifty years. It is no surprise that the beanbag made an entry to the workplace after all these years.

Similarly, if the context involves allowing workers to 'feel at home', it is worthwhile identifying influencers who are conducting research on what makes workers productive, working from home. Once the insights are understood, the trick is to apply them in the context of the client organization's project.

A LAB

A lab kind of setting is what an organization needs to immerse itself into, a place where like-minded influencers with a common vision are continuously exploring. A place where quality of thinking matters, rather than a place where rapid brainstorming throws up hundreds of ideas per minute. A place that is a knowledge collective, rather than a 3-step methodology that promises success. A place that challenges the existing paradigm, rather than looking at improving the existing paradigm.

Such a lab is a place that is not dependent on the direction by a superstar consultant, but one that promotes a matrix of interactions between different influencers. The client organization needs to take on an integrative role, which besides integrating, also ensures that external knowledge is augmented with an organization's unique insights from its own network of existing relationships. The new network ensures that the discourses are not limited by the internal view and experiences.

Silent discourses around the context of the client organization's defined vision are out there. Web surfing, attending conferences and exhibitions are helpful in building a foundation. However, as this is public information, this does not ensure differentiation.

Differentiation comes from an organization's unique ability to go beyond the public discourses and identify the silent discourses before they become public and available to others. The challenge is for the organization to identify the right ones and secure an invite to the club.

Such discourses happen locally and also virtually. At iDream we dedicate about 25% of our time in research. In 2015, we set up Gallopper, a lab, which is a blend of the physical and the digital, with an aim to facilitate dialogues and experimentation. It is during immersions in such activities that we come across enthusiastic manufacturers, professors, and students, consultants who are aligned with the context we are working in; who are more than eager to share towards a knowledge collective. At times when a 'so-called' client is involved in an immersive way, it is hard to figure out who is the client and who is paying whom to be part of the discourse. Participating 'clients' often take part in such discourses by contributing experimenting ground, contextual insights and technology.

APPLICATION

There is not one best practice on how an organization needs to take part in a lab, and this is what brings in the uniqueness to the newfound meaning. What is important to understand though is that the process is exploratory and precedes the concept development stage. By that definition, setting up a new workplace comprise of three stages:

1. The exploratory lab discourse
2. Concept development
3. Design development

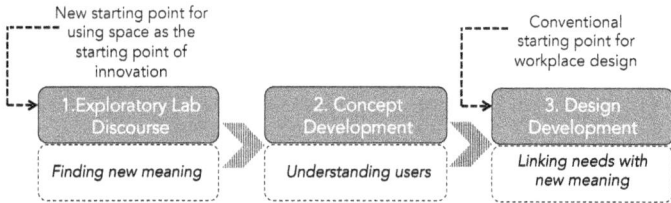

Unfortunately, a large majority of organizations like to start the process at the last stage, where outsourced teams of designers, consultants, project managers and contractors are brought in to design, develop and deliver.

The first stage of stepping back and immersing in the lab allows an organization to form a new vision. Such a vision usually gives a new meaning to things, like a new meaning about going to work itself, in context of the organization's vision. Although there is no codified way to structure the application of the learnings from the lab immersion, we have facilitated this, through a combination of interactions and workshops amongst the influencers. Paving the way to the concept stage, these workshops and interactions can be broadly sequenced in three steps of sharing, connecting the dots and selecting.

Sharing: At this step, we ask the influencers to share their interpretations in context of the said project, on the basis of their past research and knowledge. As a direct interpretation may not be always possible, we encourage the use of metaphors and analogies. We then ask them to share this with other influencers in the lab, which leads to improvement of the interpretations or new interpretations to emerge.

Connecting the dots: The next step is to identify possible options of new meanings by connecting the different interpretations. Matrices showing opposing polarities along multiple dimensions help here. Some of the emerging meanings may be closer to the existing paradigm and some may embody radical change.

Selection: An organization needs to determine its own criteria for selecting the final new meaning. As we have not approached the concept stage, it is important to keep questions related to utility and price out of the radar at this stage. Selection criteria can be defined by asking questions related to life changes, people's culture and beliefs, people's motivations and senses.

The stage that follows the immersive lab discourse is the concept stage. This stage entails understanding the user needs and this is where design-thinking principles become effective. The third stage is about design development, when one begins to explore facets like ergonomics, styling, engineering, features and technology. 'Form follows function' as an adage is relevant only at this last stage, when the approach is largely utilitarian. When this is preceded by the other two stages, designers try to map the user needs with the newly discovered meaning. Conventionally most organizations have looked at workplace design from the perspective of this third step, which is rather limiting due to the lack of alignment with the organization's vision.

PUSHING THE IDEA FORWARD

Once the new vision and the meaning are identified and aligned with each other, the project moves to the traditional phases of concept development and design development. At these two later stages, questions related to price and functionality comes up. User centricity comes to the forefront. While the lab immersion helps bring about a radical change of meaning (like new meaning for going to work), concept design helps bring about incremental value (like a smart building management system which brings down cost), and design development focuses on things, which are taken for granted (like incorporating workstations and meeting rooms). Organizations need to immerse themselves from the first stage, because the very concept of work, workers and workplace is seeing radical change.

Once an organization immerses itself into the lab frame of mind and redefines its vision and finds new meaning of work, workers and workplaces, it will find itself being a part of a collective of like-minded influencers. Because the influencers exert influence around the new meaning of work, workers and workplaces, they will individually begin to shape the sociocultural and technological scenario, creating an eco-system where the new meaning can flourish. The collective brings about a change in the way people behave, whereby they adapt to the new meaning with ease.

This book is part of that sociocultural discourse. It is sociocultural because it talks about a new language or a new meaning behind doing things. A new meaning behind the radically changing nature of work, workers and the workplace.